Re-Raising Aida
Crossing the Bridge Over Dementia

Part 1

Marilynn G. Barr

SASA™
Little Acorn Associates, Inc.

Re-Raising Aida
Crossing the Bridge Over Dementia
Copyright 2012 by Marilynn G. Barr

All rights reserved.

SASA™

An imprint of Little Acorn Associates, Inc.
Catalog No.: LAB2012FP
ISBN: 978-1-937257-14-9

Published by
Little Acorn Associates, Inc.
Post Office Box 8787
Greensboro, NC 27419-8787
USA

A mother and two daughters grapple with aging, illness, the lack and loss of memories, the reversal of parenting, and the hard resolutions.

It's about embracing the unknown; learning to adapt to the spontaneous land-scape of mood swings, the out-of-place (sometimes startling) comments and questions, the suspicion, and then finally accepting that it's not about "things aren't like they used to be," rather "everything is new," even memories are scrutinized under a new looking glass.

SASA™

Contents

How Did I Get to This Place?

The Phone Call and the Waiting

Eighty-Something Street

It Was a Stroke

The Reservations

On the Flip Side

The First Day

Our Other Sister

Evidence of Life Well Lived

What's Your Name?

Water, Water Everywhere and Not a Drop to Drink

Late-Breaking News

SASA™

Preface

Really, it's a crapshoot. The rules change everyday and each hand you are dealt often con-tains blind cards that are never revealed but you do what you can and eventually, you cross the bridge.

To all the members of my family, the many other families traveling a similar path, all the individuals who were born with the gift to care for and give more than their share or their responsibilities, and the many angels on earth who have made a difference in my journey, my sincerest thank you and blessings. You all know who you are.

I am not serving up eloquence or literary genius. What I am telling is a bittersweet slice-of-life story. There is no pause (ll). The world continues all around you. It's a matter of walking in and out of rooms, rooms familiar to you, rooms you create for a moment of gentle sleep, and rooms full of fog. All the while the world still continues, and so will you. It's not my intention to offend or frighten, rather inform, empower. If I inspire, soothe one wound, let one person know, "You will, cross the bridge." then, I am content. It's about embracing the unknown; learning to adapt to the spontaneous landscape of mood swings, the out-of-place (sometimes startling) comments and questions, the suspicion, and then finally accepting that it's not about "things aren't like they used to be," rather "everything is new," even memories are scrutinized under a new looking glass.

~

How Did I Get to This Place?

Every attempt to lose myself in the program on the screen hanging from the ceiling was fruitless. It was time for the second nitro pill and the third stick of the day with two more sticks to go. As usual, terrified of needles, I turned my head. I couldn't watch the technician poke yet another needle in to my vein to draw more blood.

The wires plugged in to the monitor and attached to wires laced through a hole and under my hospital gown prevented me from moving freely. I avoided looking at the constantly blipping graph on the monitor. Instead, I stared at the narrow row of windows hugging the ceiling that informed me it was late. I could see Gene sitting in the recliner, expressionless. I knew he was overcome with worry and I worried that he hadn't had anything to eat since early morning. He struggled not to bombard me with questions but I knew they would come. He chose his words and

pitch, which was usually bold and bass, carefully and began asking for answers to questions he didn't really want to know the answers to. In an instant, I started unraveling. There were no limbs to break my fall, no boundaries that would hold back the flood of tears from spilling out of me. And all l kept asking myself was, "How did I get to this place?"

~

The Phone Call and the Waiting

A distant but familiar noise reeled me in from an already interrupted sleep. The cell phone on my nightstand was ringing. My eyes strained to find the red glowing numbers in the dark, the numbers on the cheap digital-clock-radio, at the end of the vintage sewing machine cabinet, in my bedroom.

I love vintage furniture. It's classic and practical and every piece had a determined purpose. Some years ago I scrounged around in thrift, second-hand, and antique shops (the ones off the beaten path) for unusual finds I thought would mesh with the mismatched collection of used and hand-built pieces crafted by Gene.

I kept blinking trying to force my eyes to focus. Seven o'clock. I couldn't decide if it was morning or night. Was this a dream? My mouth was so dry, I couldn't produce a drop of spit, and my voice betrayed an obvious I-just-woke-up tone. Although disoriented, I managed a raspy "Hello."

"Listen, I'm going to mom's. The building manager at mom's building just called as I was on my way to work. She said mom called her complaining that there was a woman sleeping on her sofa and a few days ago there was a loud party in the next apartment. And that a man entered her apartment, announced he was there for the party and invited her to join the club, a club for older people where they got together for parties and go on trips. Evidently she was hallucinating. When management got to her apartment she refused to let them in." I couldn't grasp what I was hearing.

Confused, I replied with a single word, "What?"

"It's okay. Don't worry. I'll call you when I get there." My sister's voice was calm. Once before Sallie had to deliver bad news. It was April 15, 1979 when she and other family members debated whether to call and tell me our father died. She knew on this day her unexpected, early morning call would alarm me. She knew me well. Thirty-some years later, even though she masked her concern with a mellow reassurance, I knew this event would change our lives forever.

Pacing from the bedroom to the den, through the kitchen, dining room, and living room over and over again, reminded me of a fox we, Gene and I, once saw on Battleground Avenue. It walked in circles after a car had apparently hit it. But pacing didn't offer any comfort.

For nearly twenty years I asked my mother to move to North Carolina to live near me. Every time she refused. Her standard answers included, "I don't drive." "There are no buses or trains for me to go places." and "What would I do there?" She never shared any details about her life with us. Aida was fiercely independent. Questions about her finances, social life, relationships, travel activities went unanswered. Even her history, who our grandfather was; who Mr. D. was; where we lived; who we lived with; when, how long, and why we ended up in Puerto Rico; who the tall, dark, and handsome man who sported black hair, a black mustache, a sleek dark suit, and drove a Cadillac was—yes, the black Cadillac that took my sister Sallie, away from me; why mom spent time in a convalescent home; why she chose to send us away to boarding school, and why she was admitted to the hospital in the mid 1960s still remained a mystery.

~

Eighty-Something Street

Aida was a beauty. She was always impeccably dressed—coordinated colors and textures, not a single wrinkle, spot, or speck; no missing buttons; no tears or frays violated her image. One Sunday morning, while kneeling in the pew next to her, I looked up at her while she prayed and thought, "I want to look just like her

when I grow up." She wore a pillbox hat with delicate netting shading her eyes and a smart black skirt suit with a white collar. Though quite young I cataloged her style as classic. Her lips were ruby red. Her hair was short with gentle waves. Black silk stockings with straight seams in the back and black patent leather high heels accentuated her legs. Her signature beauty mark on her left cheek, just above her smile, completed the image of a graceful lady.

My mind raced through a patchwork series of memories and settled on the night we were burned out of our studio apartment on eighty-something-street near Riverside Drive.

~

Brownstones were originally one-family homes some with three floors and some with four. One floor was for the parlor to greet guests; one for the kitchen and 'the help;' one for sleeping quarters, and if there was a fourth floor, it was used for storage, called a "trunk" room. Our brownstone faced south on the west side of Manhattan. It had four floors but it was no longer a one-family dwelling. The rooms on each floor were converted in to efficiency or studio apartments.

Our efficiency apartment was on the second floor and faced the front of the building. I have no recollection of walking up or down the steep flight of stairs, however if memory serves me, our apartment was just at the top of the stairs on the right.

The door opened in to a large room with high ceilings; a pair of French doors in the

center of the opposite wall; two windows on the left wall faced the street; a wee-tiny kitchenette at the far right corner, and a tiny bathroom to the right of the front door. A Murphy bed was hidden behind the French doors. Our mother slept on the Murphy bed. Just to the left of the front door was a rectangular rod attached to the wall and supported with an anchor wire from the ceiling. A chenille curtain hung from the rod to create a sleeping chamber for Sallie, my older sister and me, where we lay our heads on opposite ends of a narrow bed.

Bedtime came early. Everyday, day-light streamed through the shear curtains when we were getting ready for bed. Aida was busy in the kitchen and shouting directions. "Wash your hands, brush your teeth, and use the bathroom. It's time to go to bed." It was a

ritual. Sallie went to the bathroom first. I sat and waited on our bed until she was done.

I didn't like it when the door was closed, so she left the bathroom door ajar when she left the room. I could hear her talking to our mother in the kitchen. Still quite small, my feet didn't reach the floor, and I could swing my legs as I sat on the toilet. I remember thinking, "It's not easy to go, when you don't really feel like going."

I sat swinging my legs back and forth and I looked around. A curtain of water covered the white tile wall to my right. The water was coming down from the ceiling. I called to my mother once, twice, three times. She finally came. I could tell she was irritated, so I immediately pointed to the wall. She gasped. I watched her profile turn upward towards the ceiling. Moving quickly, she took

me off the toilet, told us, Sallie and me to stay in the house, and then shut the apartment door behind her. There was shouting and the sound of footsteps racing past our apartment door and up and down the stairs. Suddenly the door flew open. Mother was giving instructions to her sister, Ramona, to get us out of the building, and then she disappeared up the stairs.

A long time passed until I saw mother again. I looked up at the brownstone. A fireman was on an extension ladder facing the front. It was beginning to make sense to me. "There was a flood in the building and the firefighters were drying it up by spraying fire on the building." All of a sudden, I remembered that my toys, especially my doll was still inside. I worried, would the firefighters save my doll?

It was getting dark. Sallie and I stood in the barricaded street a safe distance from the fire trucks. I took in the surreal scene in a slow motion sweep, the swell of water on the ground rushing this way and that, the firefighter directing the hose emitting fire, the water blasting out of the building, the crowd looking up at the brownstone from the sidewalk, then I saw mother. She collapsed to her knees. I couldn't hear her crying, but I could see her wailing, sobbing, lurching back and forth, in anguish. I heard someone say that she helped to evacuate the building and even carried an elderly lady down three flights of stairs. I didn't understand why she cried. I didn't understand why the firefighters were burning the flood. I wondered if they would save my doll.

~

It Was A Stroke

The sun peeking through the blinds in the den made me look at my watch. It screamed twelve o'clock. Why haven't I heard anything? What happened? I fumbled with my new "smart" phone. Press this button. No, that's the volume. Slide that button, where the hell do I get a dial pad? Though anxious, I was unusually calm when Sallie answered her phone. "Dr. Mansfield thinks mom had a stroke. I pressed him to send mom for whatever tests she needed to confirm what happened. I'm taking her to a neurologist's office for an MRI." Panic struck. My stomach tightened and my eyes felt like they were shrinking. I was paralyzed waiting for the other shoe to fall. What did this mean? I was ignorant, confused, and scared.

Waiting is a harsh taskmaster. I felt like I was trapped in a gyroscope spinning out of control. Thinking of every possible outcome. I forced myself to stay busy, to distract myself, to purge the endless "what ifs" that swallowed my thoughts.

While Aida was in the procedure room, Sallie called again and gave me more details. When she arrived at mom's apartment that morning, she found Aida wearing her clothes inside out, her lipstick was smeared around her lips, her eyebrows were thick brown arches like a clown's, and her hair was no longer a work of art but a matted mass stiffened with a helmet of hair spray. At the ready, although Sallie was shaken she remained in control. She drove Aida, in all her glory, directly to Dr. Mansfield's office.

And I knew I would be on a flight very soon.

The Reservations

Reluctantly and after long discussions, Gene and I agreed that he would stay home and I would call him and Jason, my son, to New York if the situation turned out to be more serious. Although each of us accepted a trip might be necessary, we all silently wondered how we would manage as we were all financially strapped. Plotting my exit, when, and how long, it seemed reasonable that I could do my homework in New York since I was taking online classes. I could go to the tenth floor to access the building's Wi-Fi (wireless local area network) service to do research until 10pm, read during the night while mom slept, invite her to draw with me, and email my assignments. Yes, it was doable. A little over two weeks, that would give us time to get to and from doctor appointments, make big decisions on how to maneuver through this new challenge, and if I had to stay longer, I knew Gene wouldn't be content but would understand because this was an

emergency. I made my reservations with no idea of what was really ahead.

One more charge on my already exploding credit card paid for the airline tickets. Unlike a decade or more ago, we live in a time where purchasing an open-return ticket is nearly impossible and cost prohibitive not to mention it's like playing a game of chance if you wanted to return on a specific day with short notice. The flight was scheduled to leave before the sun rose. Deciding what to pack and for how long was a comedy. I was reduced to essentials, which included minimal clothing and personal items. My books, laptop, all the cords to charge all the devices, because of course I had to stay connected, and my blanket became the precious cargo.

Precious cargo, now that's an interesting phrase but what does it really mean?

The year was 1954 or so I've been told. It was my first flight. Was Sallie traveling with the babysitter and me or was she already in Puerto Rico? I wonder. Was the babysitter a relative, a friend, or nearly a stranger? We will never know. What we do know is, I, was precious cargo, Aida was a single mother, a life condition that was scandalous for any woman during most of the last century, and sadly my earliest years would be spent separated from her.

I emailed my professors, ate dinner with my family, and left a list of telephone numbers and addresses, just in case. My itinerary was on the kitchen counter for Gene. He promised to take good care of himself while I was away.

It was the night before The First Day.

On The Flip Side

"Oh my gah!" That's the phrase that made us laugh till tears swelled in our eyes. I would repeat these words when tension was so high that the snap could put out your eye, and it always worked. Except for the fact that Aida is slowly slipping away and is no longer at the helm, her inventory of anecdotes and her spontaneous sense of humor pop in to my world and make me chuckle. Then there were times when we made her laugh.

Washing dishes was a hated chore, among others, but this was the worst. Actually no one relished the idea of scrapping the smeared food glazed over the plates in to the garbage can. Wow! I hadn't thought of the garbage can in years. We used brown paper bags to line the kitchen garbage can—you know, the ones that are occasionally offered to tote your more-precious-than-gold groceries home. We

were always corrected when we called it the "trash." Trash did not contain food. It was "garbage." Every evening the garbage had to be taken out of the apartment and down in the spooky elevator to the spookier basement. Sallie and I argued relentlessly about who was on garbage duty when we were home from school. We attended boarding school in what we called "up state." It seems it wasn't anywhere near "up state." It was just north of the city. Now Rochester, that is definitely "up state." Tarrytown was just a few stops on the Grand Central past Hastings on the Hudson.

The anticipation of the endless bickering over garbage duty agitated Aida from time to time. Sometimes she would order us out of the kitchen before we had a chance get started revving up the atmosphere. On those evenings, Sallie and I would pester Aida, just

short of explosion, and we'd order her out of the kitchen. Furious, she'd try to grab one of us. Instead we'd tackle her. One would grab legs, the other arms, and we'd carry her out like a stretcher. She'd begin giggling then cackling when we'd toss her on her bed. It was devilish fun.

On the flip side, how do you respond to "The worst sing about being ol' is living alone?" I wretch as I think of her fear and anxiety. How can I function worrying about her falling asleep without shivering in the night because she feels "all alone?" How can I function worrying about her in the shower? Will she be safe? Will she ever laugh again? Will she ever feel happy again?

~

The First Day

"Oh my!" That's all I repeated in my head when I first saw her. "Who was this thin woman? Why didn't I know she was so frail? How was she managing to maneuver through the wall of tourists traipsing around what used to be known as Hell's Kitchen, now transformed in to a midtown hotspot?"

Aida lived in what some called a luxury apartment community. It wasn't the tallest building in the "Big Apple" by any means but it towered over the antiquated six to eight story multi-dwelling residences built sometime in the early 1900s scattered around Hell's Kitchen. The

building was staffed with uniformed doormen, a concierge desk, a high-tech mailroom, housekeeping staff, and an indoor gym and laundry facility. A continental breakfast area was neatly tucked in to a corner room inside the tenth floor common area. A key-card opened the door to the tenth-floor atrium and was necessary to reenter the atrium from the wraparound balcony where one could walk, sit, or spy on the people-traffic on the street.

Every corner in her apartment housed a host of unfamiliar tiny objects integrated with family heirlooms. Plastic grocery bags meticulously folded in to triangles, stacks of junk mail including piles of requests for donations to multiple charity organizations, shopping bags full of other shopping bags, innumerable collections of doctor's business cards, dozens of duplicate restaurant menus, and clippings from newspapers

harking "Are You Depressed?" were scattered everywhere. And yet, despite these pockets of chaos, her living quarters were neat and respectably clean. The refrigerator, on the other hand, was filled with dozens of coffee creamers

liberated from restaurants. Tiny leftover bites of hamburgers, chicken, and deli-sandwiches, and a bounty of unrecognizable foodstuff most of which was more than ready for the garbage disposal dotted the shelves of the refrigerator.

She hugged me tightly. I had to fight back the tears of overwhelming sadness and quash the

quiver of fear in my voice. My thoughts reeled out of control. "Why isn't she in the hospital? She can't live alone. She can't live like this. What if she goes out in to the street and can't remember how to get back home? Where do we turn for help? Why the hell didn't Dr. Mansfield put her in the hospital?"

Sallie was at the ready with a loose-leaf binder spilling over with a flood of documents that included originals (and a multitude of copies) of mom's vital statistics, bank account statements, insurance policies, medical records, and a health care proxy. She made dozens of phone calls to social services, the senior centers Aida was affiliated with, elder advisors, family members (at my prodding), clinical trial offices for medical records, and eventually was able to make appointments to tour facilities for seniors in Manhattan, New Jersey, and Brooklyn. The

facilities she contacted were recommended by a national advocacy organization for seniors and their caregivers.

After speaking to one representative, we got the name of an eldercare advisor who specialized in investigating financial eligibility for Medicaid benefits. Another suggested resource was a freelance registered nurse who was licensed to administer an evaluation required for nursing home placement and qualifying for Medicaid benefits as well. Yes, fees were required and paid, advice was given, and reports were written. Although friends and relatives were as shocked, as we were, that hospitalization wasn't suggested, they encouraged us to hospitalize mom. Ignorant, we followed the course dictated by those we believed were experts.

Then we discovered we didn't have Power of Attorney.

~

Our Other Sister

Grace, our closest childhood friend, the one we grew from silly school girls to grown women with children has always been more a sister than a friend. As a matter of fact on several occasions she spoke for each of us, Sallie and me, at different times of our lives, to defend and honor us and we each considered her, our other sister.

Memories stored in crisis mode are chaotic and often difficult to recall in sequence without overlapping.

It's like playing "Pick-up Sticks," a childhood game we often played. If you're not familiar with this game, let me try to explain. The game pieces are a number of long (maybe 10 inch) sticks, pointed on each end in a variety of primary colors, similar to

giant toothpicks (once made of wood, now made of plastic). The first player takes the entire bunch in one hand, and from about a foot up in the air, drops them onto a flat surface. The scattered array is intertwined with sticks lying over, under, and beside each other with some trapped on top, in the middle, and at the bottom of the pile. The goal is to remove one stick at a time without moving any others. The player who could manage to take command of her own heartbeat and had nimble fingers was always able to extract one, two, three sticks from the pile without disturbing the chaos.

Pardon me. I fear I'm taking this runaway train off track.

Sallie and I waded through the chaos, one scrap of paper, one sugar packet, one cookie tin, one pile at a time. Chaos was certainly the word of the day but "carefully cataloged" took precedents. Aida's prescription information and warning sheets from the pharmacy were neatly divided, stacked, and secured with rubber bands in a shopping bag in her closet. These documents dated back to 1992. There were hundreds. Occasionally it felt like a treasure hunt. We'd stop to enjoy the scenery when old photographs, report cards, and other memorabilia popped out of the rubble. Then we returned to the sobering activity that screamed, "It's the end of an era."

We covered almost every topic of consequence on how to proceed and realized we didn't have a power of attorney. The single document, crucial to obtaining additional information and making small and big decisions concerning Aida was absent and probably had never been drafted.

At that moment, above all else, we needed an attorney.

"Isn't Gage an attorney?" I interrupted Sallie as she feverishly worked to organize the information she'd gathered. Her expression went blank. She had no idea. Again, I pressed a button on my "smart" phone. No, that's not it. After pressing the other button, I slid the screen button and finally found the dial pad but I didn't have her number memorized. Damn, where is my list of contacts. Eureka, I found my contacts list and her number. Grace answered, I told her I was in New York and what was happening. She sensed the urgency in my voice so we didn't waste time with catch-up conversation. I asked her, if Gage was an attorney and if she thought he could draft a Power of Attorney for us. A few more comments back and forth and she said she had an idea. Uncertain, yet optimistic, she ended the call. "I'll call you back in a few minutes."

Evidence of a Life Well Lived

The telephone lines were scorched day and night since September. It's now a new year and the self-imposed schedule to achieve a goal I set for myself was ticking away. We were desperate to find answers, big ones, little ones, even the ones lost in both my mother's memory and those that died with Manuela Casalduc Gonzalez, our half Spaniard, half Taino grandmother. Wrestling with the task of providing a fruitful life for someone who sporadically didn't know who we were, what year it was, and where she was, drained my

energy. Gnashing my teeth so tightly while I slept that I woke up every morning with a headache emanating from my jaws; aware that food (any food) held no appeal; losing interest in spending time with anyone including the most precious members of my family (my grand daughters) who brought light in to my life, I knew it was time to see if this boat would continue to float with all of its passengers on board. I made an appointment for a "mini-physical."

Gene didn't attempt to go with me in to the exami-nation room as he did on a prior occasion.

Height, weight, temperature, blood pressure was the traditional order of induction at the doctor's office. "No, I don't take any medications. Yes, I still take vitamins." Again, my feet didn't reach the floor as I waited for a knock on the door. "So, what's going on?" Dr. McCarty inquired. I found myself stuttering. It was a new condition.

My answers to a series of questions prompted additional tests and "You'll be here a little while."

I asked Gene to join me in the examination room and shared the "highlights" of my conversation with Dr. McCarty. I felt numb, listless, unwilling and unable to care about what was happening. I just wanted to go home.

"Do you feel any different? Did the pain go away?" Although my left arm still felt different, it wasn't the same dull pain deep in my left breast, radiating to the underside of my left arm that traveled all the way down to my middle, ring, and pinky fingers.

A single nitro pill after an EKG smoothed the strange discomfort in my arm. Gene got his instruc-tions—"Go straight to the hospital on

Church Street. They will be waiting for you. If she gets worse before you get there, go to the closest hospital."

Limp, I watched the landscape change outside of the passenger window. My thoughts drifted. She lived a good life, Aida that is, in spite of a "hear-say" turbulent history. Sallie discovered photographs, documents, objects, articles, and souvenirs in box after box she managed to salvage from Aida's apartment. Theater programs, photographs from cruises, of trips to South America, seasonal celebrations, costume parties, and more from these boxes that now devour Sallie's living space—

This is evidence of a life well lived, isn't it?

What's Your Name?

Sallie left late in the evening. We were both emotionally exhausted. I haven't spent the night alone with mom for several decades. Even when I visited New York, I stayed on Staten Island and Sallie would bring mom to her house for the duration. I worried about how the night activities would play out. Mom and I looked through a box of cards she'd received over the years, listened

to the radio, watched a bit of television, then she began a steady line of interrogation about family members. Did I ever meet Albert? Did I know her daughter Sallie? Where she lived before? Where I went when I was little? And why I left? She continued questioning me as she casually rifled through stacks of papers asking if I knew where she lived before? Albert was my father. Sallie was my sister. She lived on 111 Street between Broadway and Amsterdam. I didn't go anywhere when I was little except boarding school, and I left when I got married.

Armed with literally no information about strokes and how they can and often do affect the mind, I was crippled. I had no informed script to follow. A hint of distrust was growing. I wondered when and where it would reach full bloom. Flying by the seat of my pants with a lifetime of memories still vibrant in my mind, I began the

journey with Aida.

Aida and I prepared for bed. The moss-green love seat was actually a foam rubber foldout bed that rested on the floor. At this point I didn't care where I slept. A cot, the bare floor, a plank, a rock bed would suffice. I was spent. I had my blanket. I crocheted it years ago. It was heavy but comfortable. The spaces between the stitches created a vent system that kept the cool or hot air out and held or released my body heat. I struggled to create distance from the clutter all around me. I folded my clothing and placed them along with my personal items, jewelry, toiletries, and the like in my suitcase. This was a two-fold activity, one to keep track of my own things and two, to make sure Aida didn't confuse my stuff with hers.

Mom retired to her room and I settled on the floor with my pen and notepad (an antiquated pair indeed). My cell phone was plugged in.

I placed it under my pillow to make sure I'd hear it if asleep. All the lights were off except the one on the antique table beside the loveseat.

The table was one of three nesting tables with French curve legs and a glass insert that protected the delicate carvings on top. The lamp survived years of rough housing in the living room on 111th street and two moves, first to senior housing on 73rd street, then here to this luxury apartment. It was the color of bleached linen with a rainbow pearl glaze.

It was a challenge to make the old, oxidized on/off switch connect. Aida had a delicate touch. She could place objects in precarious positions that made one wonder why the hell they didn't fall over. I struggled to find that sweet spot, turning the switch, to turn on the lamp but she knew exactly how much twist was required to

engage the bulb. Finally on, the lamp had a low watt (maybe 25 watts) bulb to help me strain my eyes while I tried to read. Aida also moved like a cat. I was startled when I saw her fingers grabbing the corner of the wall that separated her room from the living area. With her head peeking around the corner she asked in Spanish, "¿Que es tu nombre? (What's your name?) I imagine my eyes betrayed my startled confusion but Aida took no notice. She was intensely focused on her investigation. Her eyes were black, almost sinister. Her tone was suspicious. "Marilynn." I answered. "What is your full name, your name from before?" she prodded again in Spanish. "Marilynn Grant Barr." I answered. Puzzled (and nervous), I tried to look beyond this distrustful mask. My mind reeled. What if she really doesn't recognize me? What if she wakes in the middle of the night and doesn't remember I'm her daughter?

Oh my, what if she decides I'm a stranger and decides to swing a hammer at my sleeping head? Still hugging the corner Aida commented, "I had a daughter named Marilynn but her last name was Acosta." Her eyes and expression didn't display confusing but rather absolute certainty that I was not her daughter. This was confirmed with the questions that followed. "How did you get in the building? Did you tell them you were related to me?" I finally got the message. The Aida I knew was lost. I just answered, "Yes." Satisfied, she said good night again and went to bed. I suppose anyone not in the room would ask why I was so nervous. Never having crossed this path, my thoughts played out a bevy of scenarios of what could happen next.

    Certain my cell phone keys were set at silent, I dialed Sallie's number. "Don't turn off your cell phone tonight. If I call in the middle of the night,

you better come to the city right now. (Though whispering I made sure she heard the firm tone in my voice.) I don't think mom knows who I am." I explained our conversations and mom's eerie questions. "I'm scared she won't know who I am and smash my head with a hammer or stab me." We both laughed with an apprehensive twist. Even though some part of me didn't really believe this could happen I wasn't taking any chances. Sleep was not a visitor this first night.

~

Water, Water Everywhere and Not a Drop to Drink

Hours upon hours of research, surfing the web, scorching telephone lines, drafting query after query letter, and endless cries for useful and practical assistance correspondences and telephone calls produced very little (usable) information or answers to our needs or questions.

What I did receive were dozens of pamphlets, telephone numbers to other organizations that shared more telephone numbers to even more organizations, and letters from government officials stating they could not help, and from at least one an envelope full of, you guessed it, more pamphlets.

Aida's union healthcare insurance did not cross over state lines, however prescription coverage did. (This was not clearly disclosed until hundreds of dollars were spent.) The doctors, nurses, assisted living facilities, and other organizations that claimed "assistance," proved to be of little or no help. It's much like the hidden fees or eligibility requirements that are so small on a document most people ignore them and the less-than-30 second flash at the bottom of a television screen that I do not believe any human eye can read before it disappears. The doctors in New

York missed the boat altogether by not admitting Aida into the hospital. A confirmed diagnosis and "prognosis" was never offered nor given when asked. Senior services explained Aida "earned too much annual income" to qualify for assistances; senior living (independent or assisted) facilities cost more per month than a house payment on Nob Hill; and Sallie and I were both part-time employed with little financial resources, medical knowledge (which was probably more important than anything else), time, or space. A system of piggyback phone calls sprang from our attempts to obtain credible information. Then we entered the volleyball court dimension—our questions were volleyed back and forth between numerous agencies, health care representatives, and state and federal organizations. Everyone had a script that included "I don't know." So Sallie and I began our independent searches for information.

Foremost, we discovered that Pension payments are double-edge swords. Pensions seem to prevent many from acquiring needed additional assistance. Also, there's the "5-year look back" period. What the hell was that? Whose bright idea was this? And why was and is it necessary continues to be a mystery.

According to the dozens of research statistics I discovered, there are:

- 311.5 million people living in the United States
- 41 million are over the age of 65
- 56 million receive Social Security Insurance Benefits
- 158 million are paying in to Social Security
- 6.1 million seniors receive Medicaid assistance (qualifying is a challenge)
- 5.1 million are diagnosed with Alzheimer's or dementia
- 43% require long-term care (That's a whopping 2,193,000; at least twice more, give or take a few, than the population of Rhode Island, Delaware, Vermont, or New Hampshire to name a few.)
- A family of four is not allowed to earn more than $22,050 per year to qualify for state assistance. Let's see, that's $5,512 per person per year and approximately $15 per day, and a 50¢ per hour wage. This sounds like early 1960s wages.
- An individual is not allowed to earn over $7,000 per year, which equates to $19 per day with an approximate wage of 60¢ per hour.
- And there are nearly 50 million citizens who remain without any health insurance at all. Let's see that's approximately 1/7 of our population.

America is surely better than this.

(Note: The numbers listed above are not statistically accurate. They are the result of my search for "information." Finding so many variances, I calculated a set of means from a wide range of reported statistics found on the world-wide-web. Please keep in mind these figures vary not only from year to year but also from reporting agencies, and state to state. "Why?" you ask. Generally, I believe because these figures deal with the pulse of "real" people. So, I will temper my opinions from time to time.)

I imagine you're thinking right at this moment, "Why not just move Aida in?"

These conversations will continue in Part 2.

~

Late-Breaking News

I lay on the gurney in the hallway waiting to be moved in to a room. I was presented with a choice by the doctor on call, either stay overnight or opt for a truncated series of tests. I opted for the latter. There was no way I was staying in the hospital all night. I was sleepy, hungry, and cold but even though worry was buried somewhere inside of me, I couldn't begin to imagine how Gene felt. He'd been up since five in the morning. "Did we eat breakfast?" I wondered. Even so, I knew he had to be tired and hungry aside from worried. His body ached all the time now. I worry each month waiting for the PSA test results. "Will the number be the same? Will it double? Will his bone cancer spread? Will the chronic lymphocytic leukemia he was diagnosed with last summer, progress to full blown leukemia?"

These questions continue to haunt me since his prostatectomy nearly eight years ago.

~

Worry, what a concept. I lecture others that worry is wasted energy. "Stay busy. Get involved in some physical activity..." Those were some of the "sage" words that escaped from my lips to just about anyone who was engulfed by difficult circumstances including illness, financial hardship, fear of some imminent danger or event. I've always known those words. Sometimes I heed my own advice and sometimes the sage words give me no satisfaction. Nevertheless, worry still plagues me but in a new dimension. There are no rules here, no instructions, there are no holds barred. It's an all-out assault on my senses and so here I lay with the late-breaking news that this boat is sinking.

~

The End of Part 1

Re-Raising Aida—Part 1

Crossing the Bridge Over Dementia

© 2012 Marilynn Barr

SASA™

An imprint of Little Acorn Associates, Inc.

Catalog No.: LAB2012F

ISBN: 978-1-937257-04-4

Part 2 anticipated release date:
December 2012/January 2013

www.ingramcontent.com/pod-product-compliance
Lightning Source LLC
Chambersburg PA
CBHW041815040426
42451CB00001B/2